100

Restaurant
INTERIORS

GLOUCESTER MASSACHUSETTS

ROCKPORT
PUBLISHERS

5/0

For more beautiful work by these designers and others, see these books, also from Rockport Publishers:
Commercial Lighting, by Randall Whitehead
Hotel Design
Hotels: International Design Portfolios, by Elena Moreno Marcheso
Interior Color by Design: Commercial, by Sandra Ragan

First published in the United States of America by:
Rockport Publishers, Inc.
33 Commercial Street
Gloucester, Massachusetts 01930-5089
Telephone: (978) 282-9590
Facsimile: (978) 283-2742

Distributed to the book trade and art trade in the United States by:
North Light Books, an imprint of
F & W Publications
1507 Dana Avenue
Cincinnati, Ohio 45207
Telephone: (800) 289-0963

Other Distribution by:
Rockport Publishers, Inc.
Gloucester, Massachusetts 01930-5089

ISBN 1-56496-485-X

10 9 8 7 6 5 4 3 2 1

Designer: SYP Design & Production
Cover Image credit: see page 25

Printed in China.

Introduction

Restaurant design is akin to theater design: it sets a stage, effectively creating the mood for a whole dining experience. While a cup of coffee is just a cup of coffee, the surroundings in which that steaming cup are served subtly engage the diner, and can offer a tenor that ranges from hard-edged urban sophistication to upscale elegance to downplayed comfort.

The way designers convey the soul of a restaurant is a complex affair, dependent upon factors both concrete and visceral. Like ingredients in a well-orchestrated dish, choices in lighting, graphic design, colors, fabrics, wall and floor treatments, furniture and fixtures must blend into a perfectly palatable whole. Whether the personality of the ultimate "dish" projects high-concept urban sophistication or downhome comfort, intimacy, or grandeur, the diner must feel him- or herself part of some greater drama; one that adds spice, and interest, to the daily business of eating.

Design Aiello Associates, Inc.
Project Terra Bistro, The Vail Athletic Club
VAIL, COLORADO

PHOTO: PHILLIP NILSSON

Design The International Design Group
Project La Colonnade
METRO CENTRE, GATESHEAD, UNITED KINGDOM

A travertine marble floor with inset deep blue ceramic diamond tiles laid in a Genoese pattern continues the theme. A central raised ceiling lit by cornice lighting emphasizes the light and airy mood of the space. A colonnade of arches form the surrounding surfaces and completes the framing of the restaurant and bar.

PHOTO: PHILLIP NILSSON

Design Jessica Hall
Lighting Randall Whitehead and Catherine Ng
Architect Huntsman Associates
Project Regina Chi Chi Beignet
SAN FRANCISCO, CALIFORNIA

Playful "cukoo's nest" pendant fixtures by Christina Spann invite diners into the party-like atmosphere of this space. A framing projector creates a star pattern at the far end of the restaurant, the visual reward for making the long trip from the front door.

Design Aiello Associates, Inc.
Project Terra Bistro, The Vail Athletic Club
VAIL, COLORADO

PHOTO: PHILLIP NILSSON

Design Alan and Joy Ohashi
Lighting Alan and Joy Ohashi
Architect Alan and Joy Ohashi
Project Sushi Kinta Restaurant
SAN FRANCISCO, CALIFORNIA

Located near a busy pedestrian thoroughfare,
a twelve-foot long, neon-lit fish sign attracts
passersby. Bronze-colored mirrors and focused,
high-key, low-voltage, cable-mounted lighting
enhance the surroundings without distracting
diners. The use of white plastic laminate and
maple cabinets creates a sense of cleanliness,
order, and simplicity.

PHOTO: JOHN SUTTON

Design Paul Haigh, Barbara H. Haigh
Lighting Paul Haigh
Architect Haigh.Architects.Designers
Project Caroline's Comedy Club
NEW YORK, NEW YORK

This view of the free-standing bar tables, positioned below recessed down-lights, shows the elliptical shape of the stone table tops projected onto the terrazzo floor.

PHOTO: ELLIOT KAUFMAN

Design Paul Haigh, Barbara H. Haigh
Lighting Paul Haigh
Architect Haigh.Architects.Designers
Project Caroline's Comedy Club
NEW YORK, NEW YORK

This detail view of the drinks rail at the rear of the theater shows an uplight projection onto the concrete wall.

PHOTO: ELLIOT KAUFMAN

Design Paul Haigh, Barbara H. Haigh
Lighting Paul Haigh
Architect Haigh.Architects.Designers
Project Caroline's Comedy Club
NEW YORK, NEW YORK

The seating tiers of the club are accented with fiber optics, and the "Caroline's" sign is highlighted with three-color bank lights.

PHOTO: ELLIOT KAUFMAN

Design Paul Haigh, Barbara H. Haigh
Lighting Paul Haigh
Architect Haigh.Architects.Designers
Project Caroline's Comedy Club
NEW YORK, NEW YORK

A detail view of main bar showing barfly stools. The glass soffit is downlit with recessed MR16 halogen lamps. The bar fascia is washed with light from fiberoptics. The back bar display is highlighted with recessed lights.

(INSET BELOW)
This view of the main bar/lounge shows the highlighted seating and dining areas. A curved architectural soffit is delineated with fiber-optic strings.

PHOTO: ELLIOT KAUFMAN

Design The International Design Group
Project Benihana
PICCADILLY CIRCUS, LONDON

PHOTO: NIK MILNER

Design Charles Grebmeier
Lighting Donald Maxcy
Architect Kennedy Lutz Architecture
Project Harlands
FRESNO, CALIFORNIA

Lighting becomes artwork in this project. Subtle colored gels were used behind glass-block chair rails and block windows. A suspended low-voltage track system brings light down into the dining space and counter areas. The floating serpentine elements conceal lighting over the bar.

PHOTO: RUSSELL ABRAHAM

Design Richard Foy, Mike Doyle, Lydia Young
Lighting Communication Arts/ Gallegos Design
Architect Ray Hirata
Project Wizards
UNIVERSAL CITY, CALIFORNIA

Blacklighting, special effects lighting, and exotic fabrics create the right ambiance for clairvoyance at Wizards restaurant.

PHOTO: GREY CRAWFORD

Design Di Leonardo International, Inc.
Project The Royal Abjar Hotel,
Camel Coffee Shop
DUBAI, UNITED ARAB EMIRATES

Design Di Leonardo International, Inc.
Project The Renaissance Hotel,
Main Dining Room
TIMES SQUARE, NEW YORK

The use of luxurious materials and subtle color
combinations produces a sophisticated setting.

Design Di Leonardo International, Inc.
Project The Royal Abjar Hotel,
Grand Ballroom
DUBAI, UNITED ARAB EMIRATES

Design Elias Design Group, Inc.
Project The Sheraton Carlton,
Allegro Restaurant
WASHINGTON, D.C.

Indirect lighting reflected off the 100-year-old hand-painted ceiling creates the ambiance of a sunset in Rome. The Washington Post cites this room as one of the most romantic in the nation's capital.

PHOTO: PETER PAIGE

Design Vivian/Nichols Associates, Inc.
Project Houstonian Hotel and
Conference Center
HOUSTON, TEXAS

A reference to the atmosphere of a turn-of-the-century great lodge creates an understated mountain environment, replete with natural materials, warm colors, and commissioned nature and country artwork at the Houstonian Hotel and Conference Center.

PHOTO: MICHAEL FRENCH

Design Barry Design Associates, Inc.
Project Hotel Nikko Tokyo
TOKYO, JAPAN

Two of the hotel's eleven restaurants and lounges
are shown here. The Bayside Café evokes images
of the ocean, from a tile mosaic of underwater
animal life, to lamp fixtures that conjure up
undulating seaweed and other plants. The
Toh-Gu Restaurant is a modern twist on the
traditional design of a Chinese temple.

Design Barry Design Associates, Inc.
Project Imperial Hotel Osaka

The designers were challenged to maintain
references to the original design of the
architectural visionary Frank Lloyd Wright. The
Rainbow Lounge has energetic, contemporary
designs, intended to appeal to a young clientele.

Design Design Continuum, Inc.
Project Hotel Inter-Continental
LOS ANGELES, CALIFORNIA

The creatively lighted ceiling coffers of the Grand
Ballroom nicely satisfy the requirements of both
meeting and banquet functions.

PHOTO: MILROY & MCALLEER

Design Di Leonardo International, Inc.
Project New World Hotel
MANILA, PHILIPPINES

Contemporary, sophisticated design prevails at the New World Hotel, in Makati-Metro, Manila, Philippines.

PHOTO: ARTHUR KAN

Design Einhorn Yaffee Prescott Architecture
and Engineering
Project The Equinox
MANCHESTER, NEW HAMPSHIRE

PHOTO: BILL MURPHY

Design Hughes Design Associates
Project Renaissance Mayflower Hotel
WASHINGTON, D.C.

One of Washington, D.C.'s more prominent
hotels, The Renaissance Mayflower, was recently
refurbished by Hughes.

Design Hirsch / Bedner Associates
Principal Designers Patricia Glasow and
Len Auerbach
Lighting Designer Virva Kokkonen
Architect ELS / Elbasoni & Logan Architects
Project Hyatt Regency
SAN FRANCISCO, CALIFORNIA

The Café uses a low-voltage open conductor
wire system spanning up to 60 feet. Twenty-watt
narrow spot MR 16 lamps illuminate tables, plants,
and artwork, as well as the stepped ceiling above
the atrium floor.

PHOTO: JOHN SUTTON PHOTOGRAPHY

Design Di Leonardo International, Inc.
Project New World Hotel
KOWLOON, HONG KONG

For the renovation of the New World Hotel in
Kowloon, Hong Kong, additional area above
the lobby, was secured to create a dramatic
two-volume space.

PHOTO: JAIME ARDILES, ARCE

Design Peter Gisolfi Associates
Project Castle at Tarrytown
TARRYTOWN, PENNSYLVANIA

Once an outside porch, the Terrace Dining Room
was enclosed.

PHOTO: NORMAN MCGRATH

Design The Gettys Group, Inc.
Project The Radisson Plaza
INDIANAPOLIS, INDIANA

Renovation of the Radisson Plaza in Indianapolis
has created a more unified and inviting internal
image for the hotel.

PHOTO: JOHN MILLER/HEDRICH BLESSING PHOTOGRAPHY

Design The Gettys Group, Inc.
Project The Radisson Plaza
INDIANAPOLIS, INDIANA

Renovation of the Radisson Plaza in Indianapolis has created a more unified and inviting internal image for the hotel.

PHOTO: JOHN MILLER/HEDRICH BLESSING PHOTOGRAPHY

Design Birch Coffey Design Associates, Inc.
Project The Mercury

The circular layout and flow of the café eating areas assure comfortable and efficient passenger service on the Century, one of Celebrity Cruises' newest luxury liners.

PHOTO: PHILLIP ENNIS

Design Hirsch/Bedner Associates
MAUI, HAWAII

The open air dining area is surrounded by waterfalls and tropical birds.

Design Paul Carrara
Lighting Christina Spann/Lightspann
Architect Dave Leff Construction and
Paul Carrara
Project Sapphire Mynx Bistro
SEBASTOPOL, CALIFORNIA

Inspired by the bistro's name, Sapphire Mynx, Lightspann designed a series of deep-blue blown glass orbs to illuminate and define the area around the bar.

Design Aiello Associates, Inc.
Project Embassy Suites, Breakfast Area
DENVER, COLORADO

Design Cass Calder Smith Architecture, Inc.
Colorist James Goodman Studio
Lighting Design Architecture and Light,
Darryl Hawthorne
Project Rose Pistola
SAN FRANCISCO, CALIFORNIA

This vibrant new North Beach haunt references
the neighborhood's spirited past, yet is
cosmopolitan and updated in feeling. Key
references include the colors and form of the
Italian Riviera, from which early generations of
North Beach residents originated.

Design Cass Calder Smith Architecture, Inc.
Colorist James Goodman Studio
Lighting Design Architecture and Light,
Darryl Hawthorne
Project Rose Pistola
SAN FRANCISCO, CALIFORNIA

Design Cass Calder Smith Architecture, Inc.
Colorist James Goodman Studio
Lighting Design Architecture and Light,
Darryl Hawthorne
Project Rose Pistola
SAN FRANCISCO, CALIFORNIA

Design Cass Calder Smith Architecture, Inc.
Colorist James Goodman Studio
Lighting Design Architectural Lighting Design
Landscape Design Bradley Burke
Graphic Design Spotted Dog
Project Restaurant Zibibbo
PALO ALTO, CALIFORNIA

The goal for this project was to create a casual setting with a clear sense of place that would be harmonious with the downtown urban activity and which would result in the establishment of a beloved landmark. Zibibbo is organized along a yellow brick road that runs through the length of the restaurant and passes new and existing spaces, indoors and out.

Design Cass Calder Smith Architecture, Inc.
Colorist James Goodman Studio
Lighting Design Architectural Lighting Design
Landscape Design Bradley Burke
Graphic Design Spotted Dog
Project Restaurant Zibibbo
PALO ALTO, CALIFORNIA

Design Cass Calder Smith Architecture, Inc.
Colorist James Goodman Studio
Lighting Architectural Lighting
Landscape Design Bradley Burke
Graphic Design Spotted Dog
Project Frantoio Ristorante
SAN FRANCISCO, CALIFORNIA

The Italian-styled interior and exterior were inspired primarily by the farmhouses of Tuscany. Other references and inspirations include enclosed European gardens and fine Milano modernism. An olive oil production facility is the "stage" for the dining room, and was the starting point for the project.

Design Cass Calder Smith Architecture, Inc.
Colorist James Goodman Studio
Lighting Architectural Lighting
Landscape Design Bradley Burke
Graphic Design Spotted Dog
Project Frantoio Ristorante
SAN FRANCISCO, CALIFORNIA

Design Cass Calder Smith Architecture, Inc.
Colorist James Goodman Studio
Lighting Design Architecture and Light,
Darryl Hawthorne
Project Rose Pistola
SAN FRANCISCO, CALIFORNIA

Design Birch Coffey Design Associates, Inc.
Project The Mercury

Dining and public areas were designed to appeal
to a broad customer base, one that includes
younger cruisers.

PHOTO: PHILLIP ENNIS

Design
Elias Design Group, Inc.
Project
The Sheraton Manhattan Hotel, Bistro 790
NEW YORK, NEW YORK

Not one downlight mars the hand-painted ceiling
vault. Indirect lighting is provided by miniature
sources concealed in slim, floating beams which
reflect off the colorful ceiling.

Design The Gettys Group, Inc.
Project Hilton Inn Lisle
NAPERVILLE, ILLINOIS

Sophisticated interiors make this renovated
suburban hotel distinctively different from its
nearby competition.

PHOTO: JOHN MILLER/HEDRICH BLESSING PHOTOGRAPHY

Design Cass Calder Smith Architecture, Inc.
Colorist James Goodman Studio
Lighting Architectural Lighting
Landscape Design Bradley Burke
Graphic Design Spotted Dog
Project Frantoio Ristorante
SAN FRANCISCO, CALIFORNIA

Design International Design Group
Project Skyline Hotel
CREOLE QUARTER, TORONTO

The Creole Quarter is tied harmoniously together with painted wood archways, pillars, and old world floor tiles on the walkways. Antiques and artifacts are evident throughout and lend authenticity and character to the Quarter. The moldings, railings, benches, and lamps all witness to the French influence. The Creole Quarter combines the charm and flavor of New Orleans with the efficiencies of modern merchandising and food service.

Design Design Collective Incorporated

Golden-colored walls define a large, open space in this restaurant. A deeper tone of color on the booths makes them seem even more private. The repetition of pattern and color adds to the intimate atmosphere.

PHOTO: STUDIOOHIO

Design Knauer Inc.

Project Grand Geneva Resort and Spa

LAKE GENEVA, WISCONSIN

New restaurants and a wellness spa were added to the resort, and a number of guest rooms were reconfigured to create suites.

PHOTO: JAMES YOCHUM

Design The Gettys Group, Inc.
Project Hyatt Regency
OAK BROOK, ILLINOIS

At the Hyatt Regency Oak Brook, the proximity
to Chicago drove the theme, as evidenced in the
murals and artifacts.

PHOTO: BRUCE VAN INWEGEN

Design James Marzo Design
Lighting Randall Whitehead and Catherine Ng
Project Silks Restaurant, Mandarin
Oriental Hotel
SAN FRANCISCO, CALIFORNIA

Recessed accent luminaries bring out the colors
of the painting. The custom fixtures become part
of the atmosphere, instead of overpowering or
simply fading into the background.

PHOTO: JOHN VAUGHAN

Design Elias Design Group, Inc.
Project The Sheraton Washington,
Americus Restaurant
WASHINGTON, D.C.

Situated on the atrium balcony at this convention
hotel, the restaurant provides a "see and be seen
atmosphere" for guests. The sparkle and glamour
enliven the entire lobby.

PHOTO: PETER PAIGE

Design Di Leonardo International, Inc.
Project The Royal Abjar Hotel,
Oasis Lounge Bar
DUBAI, UNITED ARAB EMIRATES

Design Rita St. Clair Associates, Inc.
Project Hotel Intercontinental Miami,
Palm Court Restaurant
MIAMI, FLORIDA

The elevated gazebo-like room is enhanced by a
lattice enclosure that screens surrounding lobby
activities. Cove lighting illuminates the artist mural
within the coffered ceiling.

PHOTO: DAN FORER

Design Di Leonardo International, Inc.
Project Stouffers Concourse Hotel
ATLANTA, GEORGIA

STOUFFERS CONCOURSE HOTEL AT HARTSFIELD
INTERNATIONAL AIRPORT, ATLANTA, GEORGIA, WITH ITS
ATRIUM GARDEN COURT AND PRIVATE DINING AREAS, IS
HELPING TO CREATE A NEW TRADITIONAL STYLE FOR
SOUTHERN HOSPITALITY.

PHOTO: JAIME ARDILES, ARCE

Design The Interior Design Group, Inc.
Project Benihana
LONDON, UNITED KINGDOM

Design Cass Calder Smith Architecture
Lighting David Malman, Architectural
Lighting Design
Architect Cass Calder Smith Architecture
Project Restaurant Lulu
SAN FRANCISCO, CALIFORNIA

The side seating area is lit by a combination of reflected uplights on the back of each column. Paintings are illuminated with custom wall-mounted accent lights.

PHOTO: MICHAEL BRUK

Design Rita St. Clair Associates, Inc.
Project Doubletree Inn at the Colonnade
BALTIMORE, MARYLAND

The Polo Grill features a compact bar entrance opening onto a multi-level dining area. Ambient cove lighting with dimmer controls creates changing levels of illumination in the windowless space.

PHOTO: MAXWELL MACKENZIE

Design Knauer Inc.
Project Grand Geneva Resort and Spa
LAKE GENEVA, WISCONSIN

New restaurants and a wellness spa were added to the resort, and a number of guest rooms were reconfigured to create suites.

PHOTO: JAMES YOCHUM

Design Hirsch/Bedner Associates
BELGRADE, YUGOSLAVIA

Intimate dining area in elegant hotel.

Design The International Design Group
Project Koffee & Cream
TORONTO, CANADA

Design Barry Design Associates, Inc.
Project Imperial Hotel
OSAKA, JAPAN

Western design was incorporated into many of the public spaces. Guests can arrange to hold their nuptials in the Wedding Chapel, dine in a classical French restaurant with a touch of modern whimsy, or attend a banquet in the grand Empire Ballroom.

Design Di Leonardo International, Inc.
Project Westin Hotel
PROVIDENCE, RHODE ISLAND

A variety of comfortable lounges and restaurants offer business guests a choice of mood during the evening.

PHOTO: WARREN JAGGER

Design The International Design Group
Project Les Colonnes
TORONTO, CANADA

Design Cass Calder Smith Architecture, Inc.
Colorist James Goodman Studio
Lighting Architectural Lighting
Landscape Design Bradley Burke
Graphic Design Spotted Dog
Project Frantoio Ristorante
SAN FRANCISCO, CALIFORNIA

Design Arrowstreet, Inc.
Project Harvard Square Hotel
CAMBRIDGE, MASSACHUSETTS

Arrowstreet's renovation of the Harvard Square
Hotel included new building systems and re-
creation of the public spaces and guest rooms,
along with a new entrance that faces onto
Harvard Square. From the street level entrance,
one enters a new two-level space revealing the
upper lobby and the lower café.

Design Design Continuum, Inc
Project Hotel Inter-Continental
LOS ANGELES, CALIFORNIA

The sophisticated club ambiance of the 211-room
Hotel Inter-Continental Toronto is derived from
warm wood tones, sparkling brass and crystal,
cool marble floors, walls and accents, and colors
of rose and moss green. This rich warmth washes
the hotel interiors from the lobby to the guest
rooms.

PHOTO: MILROY & MCALLEER

Design Hill/Glazier Architects
Project Shutters on the Beach
SANTA MONICA, CALIFORNIA

Located in Santa Monica, Shutters on the Beach recalls the historic resorts and craftsman-style cottages of the Southern California coast at the turn of the century.

Design Knauer Inc.
Project Milwaukee Hilton
MILWAUKEE, WISCONSIN

Designed in 1928 in the Empire style by Holabird and Roche, the Milwaukee Hilton had suffered years of neglect. Knauer, Inc. stepped in to reclaim the landmark hotel without sacrificing any of the original architectural details. The rich wood-tones of the lobby appear elsewhere, as in the English Room, right.

PHOTO: JAMES YOCHUM

Design Di Leonardo International, Inc.
Project New World Hotel
MANILA, PHILIPPINES

Contemporary, sophisticated design prevails at the New World Hotel, in Makati-Metro, Manila, Philippines.

PHOTO: ARTHUR KAN

Design Cass Calder Smith Architecture, Inc.
Colorist James Goodman Studio
Lighting Architectural Lighting
Landscape Design Bradley Burke
Graphic Design Spotted Dog
Project Frantoio Ristorante
SAN FRANCISCO, CALIFORNIA

Design Rita St. Clair Associates, Inc.
Project Hotel Intercontinental Miami, Lobby
MIAMI, FLORIDA

The massive travertine atrium lobby becomes
festive with overscaled umbrellas set aglow by
filtered spotlights. Triangular area rugs anchor
groupings of painted rattan lounge furniture
gathered around the Henry Moore sculpture.

PHOTO: DAN FORER

Design Cass Calder Smith Architecture, Inc.
Colorist James Goodman Studio
Lighting Design Architectural Lighting Design
Landscape Design Bradley Burke
Graphic Design Spotted Dog
Project Restaurant Zibibbo
PALO ALTO, CALIFORNIA

Design Wimberly Allison Tong & Goo
Architects and Planners
Project Prince Felipe, Hyatt, La Manga Club
LA MANGA, SPAIN

Dining rooms and other public spaces are an
upbeat mix of classic and contemporary design.

PHOTO: ROBERT MILLER

Design Ann McKenzie
Project P.F. Changs
Architect Rick Schreiber
Lighting Pam Ackerman, China Bistro
SCOTTSDALE, ARIZONA

Custom designed, floating, circular metal and canvas discs are suspended mysteriously over the dining floor. Low-voltage cable lights dash across space from statues to walls. Track lights float overhead like stars in the dark sky.

PHOTO: MARK BOISCLAIR PHOTOGRAPHY, INC.

Design AiGroup/Architects, P.C.
Project The Suite Hotel at Underground Atlanta, Dining Room
ATLANTA, GEORGIA

Original heavy bronze windows frame the delightful view that provides the backdrop for the intimate restaurant elegantly enhanced by exquisite marbles, rich mahogany millwork and hand tufted custom carpets.

PHOTO: GARY KNIGHT &ASSOCIATES

Design The International Design Group, Inc.
Project Benihana
LONDON, UNITED KINGDOM

Design Cass Calder Smith Architecture, Inc.
Colorist James Goodman Studio
Lighting Design Architectural Lighting Design
Landscape Design Bradley Burke
Graphic Design Spotted Dog
Project Restaurant Zibibbo
PALO ALTO, CALIFORNIA

Design Cass Calder Smith Architecture, Inc.
Colorist James Goodman Studio
Lighting Design Architectural Lighting Design
Landscape Design Bradley Burke
Graphic Design Spotted Dog
Project Restaurant Zibibbo
PALO ALTO, CALIFORNIA

Design Cass Calder Smith Architecture, Inc.
Colorist James Goodman Studio
Lighting Design Architectural Lighting Design
Landscape Design Bradley Burke
Graphic Design Spotted Dog
Project Restaurant Zibibbo
PALO ALTO, CALIFORNIA

Design Cass Calder Smith Architecture, Inc.
Colorist James Goodman Studio
Lighting Design Architectural Lighting Design
Landscape Design Bradley Burke
Graphic Design Spotted Dog
Project Restaurant Zibibbo
PALO ALTO, CALIFORNIA

Design Cass Calder Smith Architecture, Inc.
Colorist James Goodman Studio
Lighting Design Architectural Lighting Design
Landscape Design Bradley Burke
Graphic Design Spotted Dog
Project Restaurant Zibibbo
PALO ALTO, CALIFORNIA

Design Cass Calder Smith Architecture, Inc.
Colorist James Goodman Studio
Lighting Architectural Lighting
Landscape Design Bradley Burke
Graphic Design Spotted Dog
Project Frantoio Ristorante
SAN FRANCISCO, CALIFORNIA

Design The International Design Group, Inc.
Project La Collonade
METRO CENTRE, UNITED KINGDOM

Directory

Aiello Associates *4, 6, 25*
1525 Market St.
Denver, CO 80202
(303) 892-7024
fax: (303) 892-7039
e-mail: PPAIELLO @ aol.com

Ai Group *40, 70*
1197 Peachtree Street
Atlanta, GA 30361
(404) 873-2555
fax: (404) 875-3970
e-mail: aigroup @ mindspring.com

Arrowstreet, Inc. *58*
212 Elm Street
Somerville, MA 02144

Barry Design Associates, Inc. *15, 54*
10780 Santa Monica Boulevard
Suite 300
Los Angeles, CA 90025

Birch Coffey Design Associates *24, 38, 40*
206 East 63rd Street
Suite 3
New York, NY 10021

Brennan Beer Gorman/Architects *65, 67*
Brennan Beer Gorman Monk/Interiors
515 Madison Avenue
New York, NY 10022

Cass Calder Smith Architecture, Inc. *26-37, 42,*
49, 57, 62, 63, 72-77
522 Second Street
San Francisco CA 94107
(415) 546-6470
fax: (415) 546-6415
e-mail: Cass @ CCS ARCHITECTURE.COM

Communication Arts *11*
1112 Pearl Street
Boulder, CO 80302
(303) 447-8202
fax: (303) 440-7096
e-mail: rfoy@commarts-boulder.com

Design Collective Incorporated *43*
130 East Chestnut Street #101
Columbus, OH 43215
(614) 464-2880
fax: (614) 464-1180

Design Continuum, Inc. *16, 59*
5 Piedmont Road NE
Suite 300
Atlanta, GA 30305

DiLeonardo International, Inc. *12, 13, 17, 20, 48,*
55, 61, 68
2350 Post Rd., Suite 1
Warwick, R.I 02886
(401) 732-2900
fax: (401) 732-5315

Einhorn Yaffee Prescott Architecture and
Engineering *18*
The Argus Building
Broadway at Beaver Street
Albany, NY 12201

Elias Design Group, Inc. *14, 38, 46*
226E. 54th Street
New York, NY 10021
(212) 826-8700
fax: (212) 826-8703

The Gettys Group, Inc. *22, 23, 39, 45*
801 East Illinois Street
Suite 401
Chicago, IL 60611

Grebmeier - Roy Design *10*
1298 Sacramento Street
San Francisco, CA 94108
(415) 931-1088
fax: (415) 474-4796
e-mail: CGASID@aol.com

Habitat, Inc. *70*
6031 South Maple Avenue
Tempe, AZ 85283
(602) 345-8442
fax: (602) 730-0188
e-mail: rchabitat@aol.com

Haigh Architects *8, 9*
125 Greenwich Avenue
Greenwich, CT 06830
(203) 869-5445
fax: (203) 869-5033
e-mail: tome4u@earthlink.net

Hill/Glazer Architects *60*
700 Welch Road
Palo Alto, CA 94304

Hirsch-Bedner Associates *20, 24, 51*
3216 Nebraska Avenue
Santa Monica, CA 90404
(310) 892-9087
fax: (310) 453-1182
e-mail:" AnnaChristine@HBADesign.com

Hughes Design Associates *19*
1487 Chain Bridge Road
McLean, VA 22101

The International Design Group *10, 41, 43, 48,*
52, 53, 56, 64, 66, 78
188 Avenue Road
Toronto, Ontario. M5R 2J1
(416) 961-1811
(416) 961-9734
e-mail: studios@idgdesign.com

James Marzo Design *45*
251 Rhode Island Street #211
San Francisco, CA 94103
626-7250
fax: (415) 626-7260

Jessica Hall Associates *5*
1301 6th St. G
San Francisco, CA 94107
(415) 552-9923
fax: (415) 552-9963
e-mail: JHADesign@aol.com

Knauer Inc. *44, 50, 60*
741 St. Johns Avenue
Highland Park, IL 60035

Media Five Limited *68*
345 Queen Street
Suite 900
Honolulu, HI 96813

Ohashi Design *7*
5739 Presley Ave.
Oakland, A 94618
(510)652-8840
fax: (510) 652-8604
e-mail: ADS2000@aol.com

Paul Carrara *25*
625 Taylor St. #503
San Francisco, CA 94102
674-3877
fax: none

Peter Gisolfi Associates *21*
566 Warburton Avenue
Hastings-on-Hudson, NY 10706

Rita St. Claire Associates *47, 50, 63*
1009 N. Charles St.
Baltimore, MD 21201
(401) 752-1313
fax: (410) 752-1335
e-mail: rstclair@bayserve.net

Vivian Nichols Associates, Inc. *14*
2811 McKinney Ave., St 302
Dallas, TX 75204
(214) 979-9050
fax: (214) 979-9053
e-mail: VNAssociates@MSN.com

Wimberly Allison Tong & Goo Architects
and Planners *69*
700 Bishop Street
Suite 1800
Honolulu, HI 96813